Ooey-gooey Animals

Earthworms

Lola Schaefer

Raintree

www.raintreepublishers.co.uk

Visit our website to find out more information about **Raintree** books.

To order:
☎ Phone 44 (0) 1865 888112
🖹 Send a fax to 44 (0) 1865 314091
🖥 Visit the Raintree Bookshop at www.raintreepublishers.co.uk to browse our catalogue and order online.

First published in Great Britain by Raintree, Halley Court, Jordan Hill, Oxford OX2 8EJ, part of Harcourt Education.
Raintree is a registered trademark of Harcourt Education Ltd.

Editorial: Nick Hunter and Diyan Leake
Design: Sue Emerson (HL-US) and Joanna Sapwell
Picture Research: Amor Montes de Oca (HL-US) and Ginny Stroud-Lewis
Production: Lorraine Hicks

Originated by Dot Gradations
Printed and bound in China by South China Printing Company

ISBN 1 844 21020 0
07 06 05 04 03
10 9 8 7 6 5 4 3 2 1

British Library Cataloguing in Publication Data
Schaefer, Lola
Earthworms
592.6'4
A full catalogue record for this book is available from the British Library.

Acknowledgements
The publishers would like to thank the following for permission to reproduce photographs: Animals Animals p. **13** (Bruce Davidson); Color Pic, Inc. pp. **1** (E. R. Degginger), **8** (E. R. Degginger), **11** (E. R. Degginger), **23** (mucus, E. R. Degginger); Corbis pp. **9** (Science Pictures Limited), **23** (segment, Science Pictures Limited); David Liebman p. **4**; Dwight Kuhn pp. **5**, **7**, **14**, **15**, **16**, **18**, **20**, **21**, **22**, **23** (bristles, cocoon), **24**, back cover (both images); Rick Wetherbee pp. **10**, **12**; Visuals Unlimited pp. **6** (Steve Callahan), **17** (Arthur R. Hill), **23** (burrow, Steve Callahan)

Cover photograph of an earthworm, reproduced with permission of David Liebman

 CAUTION: Remind children that it is not a good idea to handle wild animals. Children should wash their hands with soap and water after they touch any animal.

Some words are shown in bold, **like this.** You can find them in the glossary on page 23.

Contents

What are earthworms?

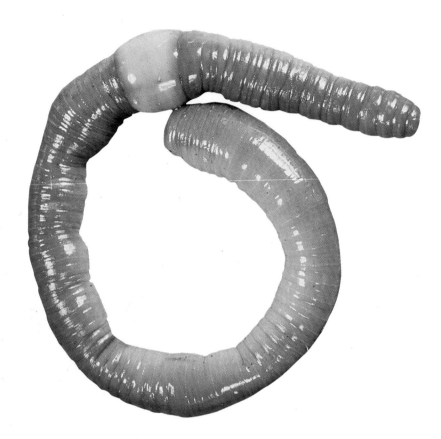

Earthworms are little animals.

They are soft, long and thin.

mouth

Earthworms do not have any bones.

They have a mouth at one end.

Where do earthworms live?

Earthworms live in the ground.

Their homes are called **burrows**.

burrow

Earthworms spend most of the time in their burrows.

They dig deep into the ground when it is cold.

What do earthworms look like?

Young earthworms are white.

Adult earthworms are dark colours, like brown.

segment

Earthworm bodies are shaped like tubes.

Their bodies are made up of more than 100 **segments**.

What do earthworms feel like?

Earthworms feel gooey.

They have slimy **mucus** on their body.

Mucus helps earthworms slide
through the soil.

How big are earthworms?

Earthworms can be smaller than your finger.

Some earthworms are massive.

Look how big this one is!

How do earthworms move?

Earthworms wiggle and push themselves along.

They use strong **bristles** to help them move.

bristles

The bristles are very, very small.

This picture makes them look big.

What do earthworms eat?

Earthworms eat dead plants.

They eat seeds, roots, leaves and stems.

As earthworms dig, they eat the soil.

Sometimes they eat an insect along the way.

What do earthworms do all day?

Earthworms are good for farms and gardens.

They mix the soil with air as they dig and eat.

cast

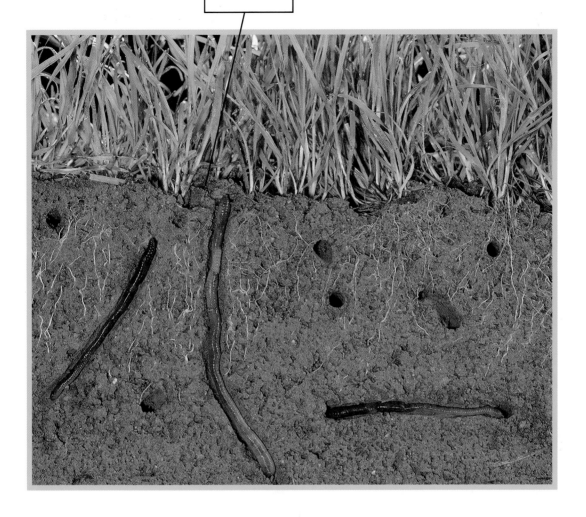

Earthworms leave little heaps of soil called **casts**.

Where do new earthworms come from?

cocoon

Adult earthworms use their **mucus** to make a **cocoon**.

It is a safe place for their eggs.

The eggs hatch.

Little earthworms come out.

Quiz

What is this earthworm part?

Can you find it in the book?

Look for the answer on page 24.

?

22

Glossary

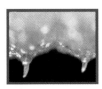
bristles
short, stiff hairs

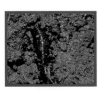
burrow
hole in the ground where a worm lives

cast
little heap of soil that worms make

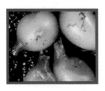
cocoon
little, hard case where worms put their eggs

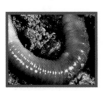
mucus
slimy stuff that some animals have in or on their body

segment
section or part

Index

Answer to quiz on page 22

mouth

Titles in the Ooey-gooey Animals series include:

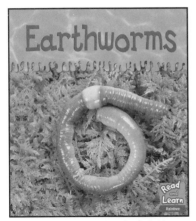

Hardback   1 844 21020 0

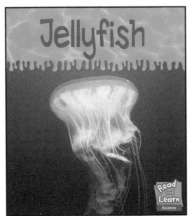

Hardback   1 844 21021 9

Hardback   1 844 21022 7

Hardback   1 844 21023 5

Hardback   1 844 21024 3

Hardback   1 844 21025 1

Hardback   1 844 21026 X

Find out about the other titles in this series on our website www.raintreepublishers.co.uk